HISTORY EXPLORERS

VIKING RAIDERS

by Fiona Macdonald

Consultant: Dr. Richard Hall

North American edition copyright © *ticktock* Entertainment Ltd. 2010
First published in North America in 2010 by *ticktock* Media Ltd.,
The Old Sawmill, 103 Goods Station Road, Tunbridge Wells, Kent TN1 2DP, U.K.

ISBN 978-1-84696-216-5
Tracking number: 3231LPP0909
Printed in China
9 8 7 6 5 4 3 2 1

Picture credits (t=top; b=bottom; c=center; l=left; r=right; OBC=outside back cover): Alamy: 4. Graham Collins: 5tl, 12t, 14, 16l. Corbis: 6, 7tr, 7cr, 8, 9r, 10–11, 12b, 13l, 19l, 19r. Richard Hall: 21br. Heritage Image Partnership: 17tl. Knudsens Fotosenter Giraudon: OBCb. FPB Photo Agency: 9tl. Universitetets Oldsaksamling, Oslo: 16–17. York Archaeological Trust: 13br, 15l, 21tr.

Every effort has been made to trace the copyright holders, and we apologize in advance for any unintentional omissions.
We would be pleased to insert the appropriate acknowledgement in any subsequent edition of this publication.

Contents

Meet the Vikings   4

Viking adventurers   6

Ruthless raiders   8

Vikings at home   10

Viking food   12

Viking fashion   14

Deadly weapons   16

Gods and heroes   18

Living in new
lands   20

The Vikings
today   22

Glossary and
Index   24

Glossary

On the last page, there is a glossary
of words and terms.
The glossary words appear
in **bold** in the text.

Meet the Vikings

The Vikings were bold, brave, bloodthirsty **WARRIORS**. They sailed from their homes in Norway, Denmark, and Sweden to attack people throughout Europe.

The Vikings were powerful for more than 300 years, from around A.D. 800 to A.D. 1100. At first, Viking warriors were led by **warlords**. Later, they were ruled by kings.

The Vikings were not only warriors— they were also skilled sailors, busy **traders**, and hard-working farmers.

Inside a Viking hall

Vikings could be rough, tough, and argumentative. But they also loved feasting, drinking, music, dancing, storytelling, jokes, tricks, and sports.

Justice, fairness, and **free speech** were very important to Viking people. They made many laws and held the world's first **parliaments**, called Things.

Viking artifacts

The Vikings were fantastic boat builders. Their **LONGSHIPS** were made from overlapping wooden planks.

Viking **CRAFTWORKERS** carved detailed designs into wood.

This **VIKING WHISTLE** is made from a swan's leg bone. The panpipe is made from wood.

Viking adventurers

The Vikings loved adventure, so they sailed away on **RISKY VOYAGES**, over stormy seas. Viking explorers hoped to become famous, take over new lands, and get rich!

The Vikings had no maps but used clouds and stars to guide them. They sailed in fast warships, powered by male rowers and by the wind trapped in the big cloth sails.

A reconstruction of a Viking warship

The Vikings sailed west and reached Iceland, Greenland, and North America.

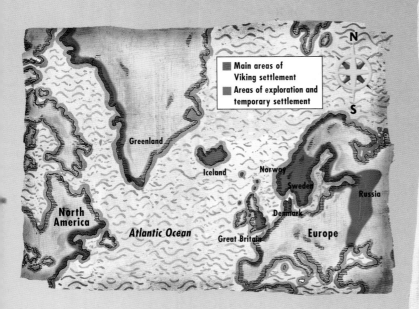

Viking traders traveled east through Russia. Sometimes they had to drag their ships behind them over frozen rivers. They traveled overland and along mighty rivers to reach **Middle Eastern lands**.

Viking artifacts

The Vikings attached decorative WEATHERVANES to their ships' masts. They showed Viking sailors which way the wind was blowing.

Rock ANCHORS kept a ship in one place when it reached the shore.

This bronze Buddha statue came to Swedish Vikings from INDIA after being bought and sold many times along the way.

Ruthless raiders

Viking meant **PIRATE!** The first Viking raiders sailed from their homelands to make surprise attacks on **trading centers** and **monasteries** close to the sea. Later, Viking pirates built camps in their new lands.

The Vikings spent the summer raiding and fighting. In the winter, they went back to their homes or rested in their camps.

A carved figurehead on a Viking ship

Viking ships had frightening monsters on the front.

During a Viking raid, no one was safe! The Vikings attacked people in churches, monasteries, towns, villages, and farms.

Actors reenact a Viking raid.

Viking raiders stole gold and silver and captured people to sell as **slaves**. They grabbed all they could, set fire to the rest, and then hurried away.

Kings in England and France paid money to the Vikings to stop them from raiding. This was called Danegeld. If a king refused to pay, the Vikings killed him.

Viking artifacts

In A.D. 1018, Viking raiders took 37 tons of silver from England as a **DANEGELD PAYMENT.**

CHARGE! This gravestone shows Viking raiders attacking with swords and battle-axes.

Vikings at home

Viking homes were usually made of wood. Most had **ONE BIG ROOM** called a hall. Outside, there were sheds for storing food and sheltering animals during the winter.

Inside, Viking homes were smelly and stuffy. They had earth floors, and some had no windows.

A reconstruction of the interior of a Viking house

Viking homes had a smoky fire in the middle of the floor and low sleeping platforms around the walls. In the evenings, Viking families listened to stories around the fire.

History experts believe that buildings like these were built for Viking royalty. They may have been used as workshops or possibly for storage.

This is a modern-day reconstruction of a Viking building.

Actors show Viking women at work.

Viking women were in charge of the home. They cooked, cared for the children, wove cloth, and made clothes.

Viking artifacts

In places like Iceland, there were no trees. So Vikings built homes made of stone and **turf**. This is a modern-day turf-and-stone house in Iceland.

Viking homes had wooden chests for storing valuables.

Viking food

The Vikings grew a lot of their food. Farmers plowed fields to grow **VEGETABLES**, such as cabbages and peas, for eating in soups and stews.

Viking farmers also grew oats and barley to make bread and beer.

This illustration shows how a Viking farm might have looked.

Viking farmers raised sheep, goats, and cows. They ate their meat, made cheese from their milk, and used their skins to make leather.

The Vikings also ate wild food. Using bows and arrows, they hunted for deer (including reindeer), wild boars, hares, ducks, small birds, and even bears.

Sea-bird eggs

Viking sailors caught seals, walrus, and many types of fish to eat. Viking boys climbed cliffs to trap sea birds and collect their eggs. Girls collected seaweed for food.

Viking artifacts

The Vikings gathered nuts, herbs, mushrooms, wild garlic, and berries in meadows and forests.

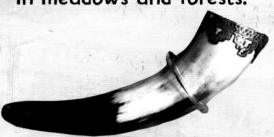

Vikings drank from wooden cups or huge cows' horns.

Querns (pairs of stones that were rubbed together) were used to grind oats and barley into flour.

Viking fashion

Vikings liked to **LOOK GOOD.** They chose bright colors for their clothes and trimmed them with fur, cord, and embroidery. Both men and women styled their hair and wore homemade makeup.

Viking men wore tunics and pants, and women wore long dresses, pinafores, and shawls. To keep warm, everyone wore hats, boots, and cloaks.

Beautiful brooches, made of gold, silver, or cheaper metals, were used to fasten clothes. Vikings also wore bead necklaces, bracelets, and rings.

Viking necklaces and beads

The Vikings kept clean in saunas. They heated rocks in a fire and then poured on water to create clouds of steam. They sat in the steam and sweated to clean away the dirt.

Viking artifacts

Viking women wore pairs of oval brooches, one on each shoulder.

Vikings smoothed their long hair with combs made from bone or deer antlers.

Warriors were given armbands as rewards for FIGHTING BRAVELY. They wore them with pride.

Deadly weapons

Vikings valued **COURAGE** more than life itself. Viking warriors joined armies led by kings and warlords and swore to loyally follow them. Warriors hoped to win glory by fighting bravely and to be remembered long after they had died.

Viking warriors fought with bows and arrows, battle-axes, spears, and swords. They wore tunics of padded leather and protected their bodies with wooden shields. Some Viking chiefs and top warriors wore **chain-mail** armor.

A berserker warrior chess piece

Berserker ("bear shirt") warriors worked themselves up into a frenzy before a battle. They put on bearskin cloaks, ground their teeth, chewed their shields, and then fought furiously.

Vikings wore metal helmets to protect their heads. The helmets had protective strips around the eyes and a nose guard.

Viking artifacts

Viking warriors gave their favorite swords vicious names such as **SHARP BITER** or **VIPER (KILLER SNAKE)**.

An ax head from a Viking battle-ax. Axes were used to **HACK ENEMIES TO DEATH.**

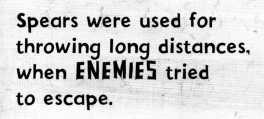

Spears were used for throwing long distances, when **ENEMIES** tried to escape.

Gods and heroes

The Vikings believed that gods **RULED THE WORLD**. Vikings **sacrificed** dogs, horses, and even people to please the gods.

Thor was the lord of thunderstorms. Vikings said he made lightning flash across the sky. Thor was very big and strong—but quite stupid!

A Valkyrie

A bronze statue of Thor

Vikings believed that Valkyries (warrior goddesses) carried the souls of dead **heroes** to Valhalla—a huge Viking hall in the sky. There, the heroes fought all day and feasted all night.

Odin was the greatest Viking god of all. Brave and intelligent, he brought victory in battle.

This Viking picture stone shows Odin riding his magic horse.

Odin rode a magical eight-legged horse across the sky. Two ravens (birds that ate the flesh of dead warriors) flew beside him. The ravens' names were Thought and Memory.

Viking artifacts

For **GOOD LUCK**, Vikings wore lucky charms shaped like Thor's mighty hammer.

This Viking **GRAVESTONE** is carved with spiked letters called **runes**. The Vikings believed that runes had magical powers.

Living in new lands

Over the years, many Vikings left their homes and looked for NEW PLACES to live. Some Vikings wanted to find better farmland. Others wanted to run their own lives, away from new, powerful Viking kings.

The Vikings settled in Scotland, England, Ireland, France, Iceland, and Greenland.

Other Vikings, called Rus, settled in Eastern Europe. The land where they lived is known as Russia today.

A Viking named Leif ("the Lucky") Ericson was the first **European** to land in North America, around A.D. 1000.

A modern-day statue of Leif Ericson

Some Vikings settled in North America, but they argued among themselves and fought with the Native Americans. They left after only a few years.

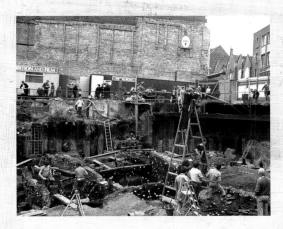

A Viking settlement was found in York, England. This picture shows archaeologists digging up Viking remains.

This is a modern reconstruction of one of the buildings from a Viking settlement in North America.

The Vikings today

Many Viking words are still used today in lands where the Vikings once settled. In English, Viking words include *sky*, *knife*, *ship*, *bang*, *birth*, *deaf*, *fang*, *freckle*, and *egg*.

Many Viking burials have survived. When excavated (dug up), they tell us about life during Viking times.

This is the Oseberg Viking ship.

This ship was found under a large mound in a field in Oseberg, Norway. A Viking queen and her servant girl were buried inside.

Some Viking activities, such as skiing and ice-skating, are still popular today. Viking hunters used skis to chase animals across snowy ground.

A Viking ice skate

The Vikings went ice-skating on frozen lakes with skates made from animal bones.

Viking artifacts

← **Birsay A 967**

Many places still have Viking names. *Birsay*, on the Orkney Islands in Scotland, means **"HUNTING-GROUND ISLAND"** in the Viking language.

Some days of the week are named after Viking gods. *Thursday* is named for **THOR** and *Friday* for **FREYA**, the goddess of love. This Viking pendant shows Freya.

Glossary

ARCHAEOLOGISTS People who dig things up to study history.

CHAIN MAIL Armor made of thousands of small metal rings linked together.

EUROPEAN A person from one of the countries of Europe.

FREE SPEECH The freedom to talk about ideas, beliefs, and opinions without fear of punishment or discrimination.

HEROES Men and women who are exceptionally brave, strong, daring, and good.

MIDDLE EASTERN LANDS Regions that are today known as Syria, Lebanon, Jordan, Israel, and Palestine.

MONASTERIES Communities of monks—men who have devoted their lives to God. They live, work, and pray together.

PARLIAMENTS Meetings to discuss the best way of running a country or community. Parliaments make laws, set punishments, and make important decisions about community life.

RECONSTRUCTION Something that is made in modern times to look like something from history. For example, a building.

RUNES The writing of the Vikings.

SACRIFICED Killed as an offering to a god or goddess.

SLAVES People who belong to someone else. They must work for their owners and can be bought and sold.

TRADERS People who make a living from buying and selling.

TRADING CENTERS Places where farmers, craftworkers, and traveling merchants meet to buy and sell things.

TURF Slabs of soil and grass.

WARLORDS Powerful men who are good at fighting. They have their own private armies of loyal warriors who fight for them.

Index

C
crafts 5

D
Danegeld 9

E
explorers 6, 7

F
farming 12
fashion 14, 15
food 12, 13

G
gods 18, 19, 23

H
heroes 18
homes 10, 11, 21

J
jewelry 15

N
names 23

O
Odin 19

R
raids 8, 9
runes 19

S
settlements 20, 21

T
Thor 18, 23
traders 4, 7

V
Viking life 5

W
warriors 4, 16, 17
weapons 16, 17
women 11
words 22, 23